www.providencebooks.net

Publisher Contact

Email:contact@providencebooks.net

Social media: facebook.com/providencebooks

Acknowledgements

The team at Providence Books would like to thank our friends, family, suppliers and customers for making our vision of creating the highest-quality books a reality. Thanks for purchasing and enjoy the quotes!

This page is intentionally left blank

This page is intentionally left blank

'Hope and change' has become a cliche in our nation, and it is daunting to think that any American could hope for change from what God has blessed.

Billy Graham

'Suffering should not make us bitter people,' my mother once said, 'it should make us better comforters.' Young people need to hear this from those who have walked before them, because someday they'll be walking those same steps, but there may not be anyone following behind.

Billy Graham

A calling is you feel - you look out and see the need - maybe it's the need for the poor, to help poor people. Maybe it's the need to get involved in the race problem, as Martin Luther King was - felt called.

Billy Graham

A child who is allowed to be disrespectful to his parents will not have true respect for anyone.

Billy Graham

A lot of Jews are great friends of mine.

Billy Graham

A real Christian is a person who can give his pet parrot to the town gossip.

Billy Graham

All my life I've been taught how to die, but no one ever taught me how to grow old.

Billy Graham

Almost everybody will listen to you when you tell your own story.

Billy Graham

As I approached my 95th birthday, I was burdened to write a book that addressed the epidemic of 'easy believism.' There is a mindset today that if people believe in God and do good works, they are going to Heaven.

Billy Graham

As I got older, I guess I became more mellow and more forgiving and more loving.

Billy Graham

As a former resident with strong personal and ministry ties to the North Star State, I pray that the good people of Minnesota will show their support for God's definition of marriage, between a man and a woman.

Billy Graham

Auschwitz stands as a tragic reminder of the terrible potential man has for violence and inhumanity.

Billy Graham

Being a Christian is more than just an instantaneous conversion - it is a daily process whereby you grow to be more and more like Christ.

Billy Graham

Believers, look up - take courage. The angels are nearer than you think.

Billy Graham

Certainly a woman should never disguise the fact that she is a woman. A woman's body is very beautiful.

Billy Graham

Christ was God in human flesh, and He proved it by rising from the dead.

Billy Graham

Christians are not limited to any church.

Billy Graham

Christmas means a great deal to me. I was reared in a family that celebrated Christmas to some extent, but I married into a family that celebrated Christmas in a big way. And my wife always made a big thing of Christmas for the children. We have five children, and we had a terrific time at Christmas.

Billy Graham

Comfort and prosperity have never enriched the world as much as adversity has.

Billy Graham

Communism has decided against God, against Christ, against the Bible, and against all religion.

Billy Graham

Communism is a religion that is inspired, directed and motivated by the Devil himself who has declared war against Almighty God.

Billy Graham

Courage is contagious. When a brave man takes a stand, the spines of others are often stiffened.

Billy Graham

Death wasn't part of God's original plan for humanity, and the Bible calls death an enemy - the last enemy to be destroyed.

Billy Graham

Don't be misled by those who claim God doesn't exist, because He does.

Billy Graham

Don't get old, if you can avoid it.

Billy Graham

Each generation faces different issues and challenges, but our standard must always be measured by God's word.

Billy Graham

Each life is made up of mistakes and learning, waiting and growing, practicing patience and being persistent.

Billy Graham

Evangelicals can't be closely identified with any particular party or person. We have to stand in the middle, to preach to all the people, right and left.

Billy Graham

Evangelism is when the Gospel, which is good news, is preached or presented to all people.

Billy Graham

Even Hubble hasn't found yet the end of this universe, and we don't know that it has any end.

Billy Graham

Even the securest financial plan and the finest health coverage aren't enough to hold us steady when the challenges come... We need something more, something deeper and unshakeable, something that will see us through life's hard times.

Billy Graham

Every President I think I've ever known, except Truman, has thought they didn't quite get done what they wanted done. And toward the end of their Administrations, they were disappointed and wished they had done some things differently.

Billy Graham

Every day is a gift from God, no matter how old we are.

Billy Graham

Every human being is under construction from conception to death.

Billy Graham

Every year during their High Holy Days, the Jewish community reminds us all of our need for repentance and forgiveness.

Billy Graham

Everybody has a little bit of Watergate in him.

Billy Graham

Everywhere I go I find that people... both leaders and individuals... are asking one basic question, 'Is there any hope for the future?' My answer is the same, 'Yes, through Jesus Christ.'

Billy Graham

For those of you who do not know Him, choosing your eternal home is the most important decision you will ever make.

Billy Graham

Freedom is relative.

Billy Graham

Give me five minutes with a person's checkbook, and I will tell you where their heart is.

Billy Graham

God has given us two hands - one to receive with and the other to give with. We are not cisterns made for hoarding; we are channels made for sharing.

Billy Graham

God has given us two hands, one to receive with and the other to give with.

Billy Graham

God is more interested in your future and your relationships than you are.

Billy Graham

God knows what we are going through when we grieve, and He wants to assure us of His love and concern. He also wants us to turn to Him and bring our heartaches and burdens to Him.

Billy Graham

God never meant that people were to wear clothes. He meant we were to be nude. But we were in a state of innocence. Then sin came into the human race and became a blood poisoning.

Billy Graham

God proved His love on the Cross. When Christ hung, and bled, and died, it was God saying to the world, 'I love you.'

Billy Graham

God will prepare everything for our perfect happiness in heaven, and if it takes my dog being there, I believe he'll be there.

Billy Graham

God's angels often protect his servants from potential enemies.

Billy Graham

God's mercy and grace give me hope - for myself, and for our world.

Billy Graham

Growing old has been the greatest surprise of my life.

Billy Graham

Heaven gives us hope and makes our present burdens easier to bear.

Billy Graham

I am amazed at the wonders of technology and am grateful for the ways in which we are able to use it to share the Gospel around the world.

Billy Graham

I am just one of many thousands called to be an evangelist.

Billy Graham

I am not going to Heaven because I have preached to great crowds or read the Bible many times. I'm going to Heaven just like the thief on the cross who said in that last moment: 'Lord, remember me.'

Billy Graham

I am well aware that there are prisoners of conscience in the Soviet Union, including some who have said they have chosen to resist the law because of religious reasons.

Billy Graham

I believe that I have received Jesus Christ into my heart. I believe that he has covered all of my sins.

Billy Graham

I believe that the greatest form of prayer is praise to God.

Billy Graham

I believe the home and marriage is the foundation of our society and must be protected.

Billy Graham

I can barely walk, but it's a privilege to be able to move at all.

Billy Graham

I can't explain 9/11, except the evil of man.

Billy Graham

I can't prove it scientifically, that there's a God, but I believe.

Billy Graham

I don't eat with beautiful women alone.

Billy Graham

I don't have freedom in the United States to go into a public school and preach the Gospel, nor is a student free in a public school to pray, or a teacher free to read the Bible publicly to the students. At the same time, we have a great degree of freedom for which I am grateful.

Billy Graham

I don't have many sad days.

Billy Graham

I don't have to see a murder in order to condemn murder.

Billy Graham

I don't need a successor, only willing hands to accept the torch for a new generation.

Billy Graham

I don't think I get angry.

Billy Graham

I don't think the Christian Right dominates America in the way some in the media believe they do.

Billy Graham

I don't think the government should be in the trailer-park business. I don't think they know how to run a trailer park.

Billy Graham

I don't think there is a single social issue I haven't spoken on.

Billy Graham

I fell and broke my pelvic bone in three places. So, I'm still sort of an invalid now.

Billy Graham

I first met Bev Shea while in Chicago when he was on Moody Radio. As a young man starting my ministry, I asked Bev if he would join me. He said yes, and for over 60 years we had the privilege of ministering together across the country and around the world.

Billy Graham

I found that this Parkinson's does slow you down, whether you want to slow down or not.

Billy Graham

I have discovered that just because we grow weaker physically as we age, it doesn't mean that we must grow weaker spiritually.

Billy Graham

I have never changed my message. I preach the Bible, and I preach it with authority.

Billy Graham

I have never talked publicly or privately about the Jewish people, including conversations with President Nixon, except in the most positive terms.

Billy Graham

I have the problems of, I must confess, old age.

Billy Graham

I haven't been faithful to my own advice in the past. I will in the future.

Billy Graham

I haven't written my own epitaph, and I'm not sure I should. Whatever it is, I hope it will be simple, and that it will point people not to me, but to the One I served.

Billy Graham

I just want to lobby for God.

Billy Graham

I kept a very full diary of my relationship with Nixon, for some strange reason, until he became president.

Billy Graham

I look forward to death with great anticipation, to meeting God face to face.

Billy Graham

I never hold a grudge.

Billy Graham

I spoke to a million in one service, in Korea, in Seoul. And that was the largest audience I ever have had.

Billy Graham

I still enjoy watching a batter successfully cross home plate, but nothing thrills me more than seeing the Holy Spirit at work in hearts as the Gospel is carried into stadiums, across the airwaves, and around the world.

Billy Graham

I think Pat Robertson is a terrific fellow.

Billy Graham

I think about my own sons and my own daughters, and I'm sure that many parents are concerned about what their children are exposed to.

Billy Graham

I think it is a sin to look at another person as inferior to yourself because of race or because of ethnic background, and I think the greatest thing to do is to pray that God will give you love for them, and I do.

Billy Graham

I think television has had a vast, unbelievable impact on us.

Billy Graham

I think that if I would talk on a political subject, if I talk about it, it would divide the audience on that issue. That's not my issue.

Billy Graham

I think that the Bible teaches that homosexuality is a sin, but the Bible also teaches that pride is a sin, jealousy is a sin, and hate is a sin, evil thoughts are a sin. So I don't think that homosexuality should be chosen as the overwhelming sin that we are doing today.

Billy Graham

I think we've taken the meaning of Christmas out. People don't stop and think about Jesus or the birth of Jesus. When they think of Christmas, they think of Santa Claus and - for the children, and they think of giving gifts and out-giving the next person of spending their time looking for the right thing for somebody who has everything.

Billy Graham

I think where political issues invade moral situations, spiritual leaders have to speak out.

Billy Graham

I used to read five psalms every day - that teaches me how to get along with God. Then I read a chapter of Proverbs every day and that teaches me how to get along with my fellow man.

Billy Graham

I want to tell people about the meaning of the cross.

Billy Graham

I was reared in the church, in the Presbyterian Church.

Billy Graham

I wish I had been home more when the children were growing up. I missed a lot.

Billy Graham

I'm going to Heaven just like the thief on the cross who said in that last moment: 'Lord, remember me.'

Billy Graham

I'm grateful for the evangelical resurgence we've seen across the world in the last half-century or so. It truly has been God's doing.

Billy Graham

I'm grateful for the opportunities God gave me to minister to people in high places; people in power have spiritual and personal needs like everyone else, and often they have no one to talk to.

Billy Graham

I'm not an analyzer. I've got a son that analyzes everything and everybody. But I don't analyze people.

Billy Graham

I'm not focused on the gay and lesbian movement.

Billy Graham

I'm thankful for the incredible advances in medicine that have taken place during my lifetime. I almost certainly wouldn't still be here if it weren't for them.

Billy Graham

I've been praying that we might have a spiritual awakening. But I think that becomes possible as individuals surrender their lives fresh and anew to Christ.

Billy Graham

I've read the last page of the Bible. It's all going to turn out all right.

Billy Graham

I've spent too much time giving speeches, traveling the world.

Billy Graham

If God doesn't punish America, He'll have to apologize to Sodom and Gomorrah.

Billy Graham

If a person gets his attitude toward money straight, it will help straighten out almost every other area in his life.

Billy Graham

If we had more hell in the pulpit, we would have less hell in the pew.

Billy Graham

If you'd have said Evangelical in 1957, most people wouldn't know what you were talking about. And then, they'd be against it.

Billy Graham

It is not the body's posture, but the heart's attitude that counts when we pray.

Billy Graham

It is well known that the Soviet Union closely regulates all organizations and movements, including religion.

Billy Graham

It seems the only way to gain attention today is to organize a march and protest something.

Billy Graham

It was a privilege to pray with Governor Romney - for his family and our country.

Billy Graham

It's no secret that in New York during the last 30 years there has been a tragic exodus from the churches into materialism, secularism and humanism.

Billy Graham

It's sometimes comical to hear the younger generation ask their peers to repeat themselves.

Billy Graham

Let me ask you a question: If you never ate a balanced diet, what would happen to your body? You know the answer: Eventually you'd grow weak; you might even open yourself to serious illness or disease. We all need a balanced diet if we are to stay healthy.

Billy Graham

Locally, I'll vote one way and nationally, maybe another.

Billy Graham

Make sure of your commitment to Jesus Christ, and seek to follow Him every day. Don't be swayed by the false values and goals of this world, but put Christ and His will first in everything you do.

Billy Graham

Man has two great spiritual needs. One is for forgiveness. The other is for goodness.

Billy Graham

Man is not born to atheism. He is born to believe.

Billy Graham

Many churches of all persuasions are hiring research agencies to poll neighborhoods, asking what kind of church they prefer. Then the local churches design themselves to fit the desires of the people. True faith in God that demands selflessness is being replaced by trendy religion that serves the selfish.

Billy Graham

Many churches today have special programs for people who are grieving, and these can be very helpful.

Billy Graham

My family is very good about visiting me, and other friends as well.

Billy Graham

My father had a dairy farm. He employed three black families and one white family, and I used to play with black children.

Billy Graham

My heart aches for America and its deceived people.

Billy Graham

My home is in Heaven. I'm just traveling through this world.

Billy Graham

My wife has about everything I can think of.

Billy Graham

My wife is already in Heaven.

Billy Graham

New York is definitely ready for the word of God.

Billy Graham

No matter how prepared you think you are for the death of a loved one, it still comes as a shock, and it still hurts very deeply.

Billy Graham

No one can outrun death. It will catch up to all of us eventually.

Billy Graham

No parent is perfect; we all can look back and think of things we could've done to help our children be better prepared for adulthood. And sometimes it's best to admit it to them and encourage them to learn from our mistakes.

Billy Graham

Nothing can bring a real sense of security into the home except true love.

Billy Graham

Occasionally I've seen children become heavy-handed and insensitive when dealing with their aging parents, and it only caused resentment and hard feelings.

Billy Graham

Old age may have its limitations and challenges, but in spite of them, our latter years can be some of the most rewarding and fulfilling of our lives.

Billy Graham

Old is authentic. Old is genuine. Old is valuable.

Billy Graham

Once you've lost your privacy, you realize you've lost an extremely valuable thing.

Billy Graham

One of the things I miss most is that I can no longer read, due to age-related macular degeneration. I get regular injections for this, and thankfully these seem to have arrested its progress, but it's still very difficult for me to read. That means it is hard for me to pick up my Bible and read it like I used to, and I miss that very much.

Billy Graham

Only God Himself fully appreciates the influence of a Christian mother in the molding of character in her children.

Billy Graham

Only God who made us can touch us and change us and save us from ourselves.

Billy Graham

Only the supernatural love of God through changed lives can solve the problems that we face in our world.

Billy Graham

Only those who want everything done for them are bored.

Billy Graham

Only when Christ comes again will the little white children of Alabama walk hand in hand with little black children.

Billy Graham

Oral Roberts was a man of God and a great friend in ministry. I loved him as a brother.

Billy Graham

Our society strives to avoid any possibility of offending anyone - except God.

Billy Graham

Over the years I've seen people lose a spouse and then withdraw and lose interest in life, and I believe we need to resist that.

Billy Graham

People have a negative impression of New York that I don't think is quite fair.

Billy Graham

Politics has always been ugly to me, and yet I accept that as a fact of life.

Billy Graham

Prayer is simply a two-way conversation between you and God.

Billy Graham

Racial prejudice, anti-Semitism, or hatred of anyone with different beliefs has no place in the human mind or heart.

Billy Graham

Racism and injustice and violence sweep our world, bringing a tragic harvest of heartache and death.

Billy Graham

Read the Bible. Work hard and honestly. And don't complain.

Billy Graham

Regardless of what society says, we can't go on much longer in the sea of immorality without judgment coming.

Billy Graham

Rose Adams is a wonderful Christian woman who cared for my mother, Morrow Coffey Graham, in her last years of life.

Billy Graham

Scripture is filled with examples of men and women whom God used late in life, often with great impact - men and women who refused to use old age as an excuse to ignore what God wanted them to do.

Billy Graham

Seemingly, man has learned to live without God, preoccupied and indifferent toward Him and concerned only about material security and pleasure.

Billy Graham

Self-centered indulgence, pride and a lack of shame over sin are now emblems of the American lifestyle.

Billy Graham

Sincere Christians can disagree about the details of Scripture and theology - absolutely.

Billy Graham

Some people spend their lives building ultimate dream homes so they can enjoy their twilight years... Others spend their last days in nursing homes.

Billy Graham

Spend more time in study and prayer. That's the secret of successful evangelism.

Billy Graham

Success is always dangerous, and we need to be alert and avoid becoming the victims of our own success. Will we influence the world for Christ, or will the world influence us?

Billy Graham

Suppose you could gain everything in the whole world, and lost your soul. Was it worth it?

Billy Graham

Tears shed for self are tears of weakness, but tears shed for others are a sign of strength.

Billy Graham

The Bible is clear - God's definition of marriage is between a man and a woman.

Billy Graham

The Bible is full of warnings about false prophets and false messiahs. These satanically inspired people have appeared in almost every generation of history.

Billy Graham

The Bible says that God has a reason for keeping us here; if He didn't, He would take us to Heaven far sooner.

Billy Graham

The Bible says that as Christians we don't grieve the same way people do who have no hope of eternity and of Heaven - but we still grieve.

Billy Graham

The Bible says today is the accepted time, today is the day of salvation... But there will come a time when it will be too late for you.

Billy Graham

The Christian life is not a constant high. I have my moments of deep discouragement. I have to go to God in prayer with tears in my eyes, and say, 'O God, forgive me,' or 'Help me.'

Billy Graham

The Gospel has never changed.

Billy Graham

The Information Highway intrigues me because I have always been a newshound; I have always been curious about why people believe what they believe.

Billy Graham

The New Testament says nothing of Apostles who retired and took it easy.

Billy Graham

The Oklahoma City bombing was simple technology, horribly used. The problem is not technology. The problem is the person or persons using it.

Billy Graham

The framers of our Constitution meant we were to have freedom of religion, not freedom from religion.

Billy Graham

The great question of our time is, 'Will we be motivated by materialistic philosophy or by spiritual power?'

Billy Graham

The greatest legacy one can pass on to one's children and grandchildren is not money or other material things accumulated in one's life, but rather a legacy of character and faith.

Billy Graham

The highest form of worship is the worship of unselfish Christian service. The greatest form of praise is the sound of consecrated feet seeking out the lost and helpless.

Billy Graham

The human heart is the same the world over.

Billy Graham

The influence of a mother upon the lives of her children cannot be measured. They know and absorb her example and attitudes when it comes to questions of honesty, temperance, kindness, and industry.

Billy Graham

The men who followed Him were unique in their generation. They turned the world upside down because their hearts had been turned right side up. The world has never been the same.

Billy Graham

The most eloquent prayer is the prayer through hands that heal and bless.

Billy Graham

The older I get, the more important the eternal becomes to me personally.

Billy Graham

The one badge of Christian discipleship is not orthodoxy but love.

Billy Graham

The only time my prayers are never answered is on the golf course.

Billy Graham

The second coming of Christ will be so revolutionary that it will change every aspect of life on this planet. Disease will be eliminated. Death will be abolished. War will be eradicated. Nature will be transformed.

Billy Graham

The thing that alarms me is that there are so many clergymen who say that the so-called 'new morality' is all right. They say we're living in a new generation; let's be relevant, let's change God's law. Let's say that adultery is all right under certain circumstances; fornication's all right under certain circumstances. If it's 'meaningful.'

Billy Graham

The time has come for all evangelists to practice full financial disclosure. The world is watching how we walk and how we talk. We must have the highest standards of morality, ethics and integrity if we are to continue to have influence.

Billy Graham

The wonderful news is that our Lord is a God of mercy, and He responds to repentance.

Billy Graham

The word 'romance,' according to the dictionary, means excitement, adventure, and something extremely real. Romance should last a lifetime.

Billy Graham

There are a lot of groups that feel a little bit strange around me, because I am inclusive.

Billy Graham

There are two great forces, God's force of good and the devil's force of evil, and I believe Satan is alive and he is working, and he is working harder than ever, and we have many mysteries that we don't understand.

Billy Graham

There have been times that I've wept as I've gone from city to city and I've seen how far people have wandered from God.

Billy Graham

There is no scriptural basis for segregation.

Billy Graham

There is nothing wrong with men possessing riches. The wrong comes when riches possess men.

Billy Graham

There's a great deal to say in the Bible about the signs we're to watch for, and when these signs all converge at one place we can be sure that we're close to the end of the age.

Billy Graham

Those outside the church expect followers of Christ to live differently, yet today many in church are chasing after the world - not to win them, but to be like them.

Billy Graham

Throughout my ministry, I have sought to build bridges between Jews and Christians.

Billy Graham

To start with, I love New York... It's a little bit of the whole world... In New York, the whole world comes to you.

Billy Graham

Traveling around the world and preaching for over 70 years did not give much time for reflection.

Billy Graham

We are not cisterns made for hoarding, we are channels made for sharing.

Billy Graham

We go on in our pleasures thinking they're going to last forever.

Billy Graham

We have an idea that we Americans are God's chosen people, that God loves us more than any other people, and that we are God's blessed. I tell you that God doesn't love us any more than He does the Russians.

Billy Graham

We're a diverse society, and I think the TV is doing a great job in showing that we're all human beings, that we can all get along, that we can all be together, and I think that's a marvelous thing.

Billy Graham

We're all sinners. Everybody you meet all over the world is a sinner.

Billy Graham

What really matters is how God sees me. He isn't concerned with labels; he is concerned about the state of man's soul.

Billy Graham

When Christians say God has been talking to them about something, it simply means they have a strong inner conviction or feeling that God has made His will known to them.

Billy Graham

When I reached 80, my world turned upside down physically. I've had a lot of physical problems.

Billy Graham

When I was young, I could not imagine being old. My mother said, and the doctor confirmed, that I had an unusual amount of energy; and it followed me into young adulthood.

Billy Graham

When anyone has the power to destroy the whole human race in a matter of hours, it becomes a moral issue. The church must speak out.

Billy Graham

When granted many years of life, growing old in age is natural, but growing old with grace is a choice. Growing older with grace is possible for all who will set their hearts and minds on the Giver of grace, the Lord Jesus Christ.

Billy Graham

When wealth is lost, nothing is lost; when health is lost, something is lost; when character is lost, all is lost.

Billy Graham

Whenever I counsel someone who feels called to be an evangelist, I always urge them to guard their time and not feel like they have to do everything.

Billy Graham

While I have never learned to use a computer, I am surrounded by family and friends who carry information to me from blogs, Facebook, Twitter, and various websites.

Billy Graham

You're born. You suffer. You die. Fortunately, there's a loophole.

Billy Graham

This page is intentionally left blank

This page is intentionally left blank

This page is intentionally left blank

This page is intentionally left blank

This page is intentionally left blank